DARLING GIRL

S. Niroshini is a writer an   in London. She received Third Prize in the Poetry London Prize 2020 and a London Writers Award for Literary Fiction. Born in Sri Lanka, she was educated in Colombo, Melbourne and Oxford and worked as a solicitor before starting to write poetry, fiction and essays.

Darling Girl

Published by Bad Betty Press in 2021
www.badbettypress.com

All rights reserved

S. Niroshini has asserted her right to be identified as the author of this work in accordance with Section 77 of the Copyright, Designs and Patents Act of 1988.

Cover design by Amy Acre

Images used courtesy of the Getty's Open Content Program and the Los Angeles County Museum of Art, and under license from Shutterstock.com (see Notes for details)

Printed and bound in the United Kingdom

A CIP record of this book is available from the British Library.

ISBN: 978-1-913268-17-6

Darling Girl

PRESS

Darling Girl

Contents

Girl, Ceylon	9
Notes on Astral Theory	14
A Bitter Plum	15
sea level	16
no more history	17
Rāga in Blue	18
Train to Polonnaruwa	19
Piranha	20
Dis-location	21
Neruda's Last Word(s)	24
period party / புண்ணியதானம்	25
Notes on Lunar Theory	27
Brihadeeswar	28
One Hundred and Eight Commands for My Daughter	30
Notes	34
Image credits	34
Acknowledgements	35

Girl, Ceylon

Albumen silver print photograph
Julia Margaret Cameron, 1875–1879

i.

Everything begins with a kiss   at the plantation   and then a disrobing
   she is sticky   in the hands   of a white woman   who lays claim to
her body
    her body   dressed in pearls   like a lady   worked to bone   like a
man   like the sons
     who put her   to bed each night   who whisper words   of the
good lord
      lord   they took her   on a dirt floor   exposed her cracked
feet

ii.

You asked me to write a poem about the history of indenture.

iii.

I am nine   and run in the wayward garden
I am nine   and pluck plumeria from undergrowth
I am nine   and catch butterflies in small boxes
I am nine   and my feet trip on swimmer crabs
I am nine   and my body is learning how to contort
I am nine   and my skin is beginning to absorb light
I am nine   and my eyes carry
all   the   water   in   the   ocean

iv.

Who cared for the body of a little brown girl in the nineteenth century? Who cares for the body of a little brown girl in the century in which I live?

v.

Albumen print, a photographic process from the nineteenth century, was developed in 1850 by Louis Blanquart-Evrard. It involved coating a mixture of egg-white and ammonium chloride on paper sensitised with silver nitrate. Toned with gold chloride, it gave the photographs a sepia hue. The troublesome weather in Ceylon however caused many problems for European photographers who relied on this process as the surface was gooey and attracted the attention of insects.

vi.

I think of the photograph when I'm at the doctor's clinic. The nurse, a young woman with strawberry-blonde hair, inserts the speculum.

I see the face of my grandmother or her mother in the face of this girl.

vii.

Daughter, let us play hide and seek
one last time:

one		run as fast as you can

one   run   as fast as you can
     two   lift your frock to avoid dirt on its fringes
three   don't trip on the roots of the rubber trees
     four   can you smell it? the ocean is not so far now
five   notice the light beyond the horizon
     six   no one can tell you're just a girl
seven   you've made it! you've made it!
     eight   strip off your dress, over your shoulders
nine   don't look back   there is no time
     ten   see the water and submerge

Notes on Astral Theory

நட்சத்திரம்	~	tamil
naṭcattiram	~	transliteration of the tamil
नक्षत्र	~	sanskrit
nakṣatra	~	transliteration of the sanskrit
nak·sha·tra	~	phonetic pronunciation
star / tar	~	what it is
fate that sticks	~	what it will do to you

A Bitter Plum

See this plum. See how this plum fits my mouth;
its furry pit revolves between my tongue until I spit it out.
I use the back of my hand to wipe my lips which wait for—

Actually my love, it's not a plum but a stone. See how this stone
fits the palm of that little brown girl's hand as she plays along the sea's
edge. Isn't she so pretty, the way she holds it with such—

Forgive me, this is really inexcusable of me. It's not a stone
but a bullet. See how this bullet travels through air, enters the abdomen
of that man with the green vest and heavy satchel—not old, not young,
with the beautiful brown eyes.

This isn't a poem about how that bullet fit my mouth, fit the palm
of that little brown girl's hand as she played along the sea's edge
and entered the abdomen of that man with the green vest and heavy satchel—
not old, not young, with the beautiful brown eyes.

It's a much, much more tangled story.

sea level

ari	aralai	aarkali	aalandhai	aazhi
ambaram	arunavam	aalam	ambonidhi	amburaasi
கயம்	கழி	கடல்	குரவை	கார்மலி
sargasso	somov	solomon	scotia	sulu
samborombón	san matias	skagerrak	szczecin	sagami
sea	sea	sea	sea	sea

16

no more history

toss a coin. a text message
alerts you to the fact that you have birthed
three daughters. one will be taken by a stranger,
another will leave forever. the last will remain with you
until your death. which is which you wonder; you become a ghost
that wanders claiming *whoo whoo*. there is no more history.
time has been vanquished by Uber Eats & breakfast TV.
you have been removed of your context, a coin that sits
on the shelf of a british museum—tetradrachm
& dekadrachm. beyond mythography, beyond
bone, you wait to die in the mouths
of your lovers.

Rāga in Blue

The Little Girl in Blue, Oil on canvas
Amrita Sher-Gil, 1934

In my dream, all I could see was blue. Blue like Peter-Rabbit's -coat-blue. Blue like the ink of my least favourite pen, picked up last winter in the doctor's room. Blue like bellflowers and sea holly on an afternoon. Blue like bruised berries, a blue dress missing its third button. Blue like the shirt Jack wore on his wedding day as he looked in my direction before he turned to face the bride. Blue like indigo, neelam and baby. Blue like the eyeshadow of the soprano in Madame Butterfly on my seventeenth birthday. Blue like the veins of the frog whose heart I had dissected in biology. Blue like a morning in Bombay listening to rāga bhairavi. Blue like the sea by my grandmother's home in which I will one day leave a part of myself.

Train to Polonnaruwa
Colombo, 1995

That summer seemed so short, standing on the roof of my grandmother's house.

A crow watches from the lane, its black eye half-sunken in pulped aubergine;

strange feast, gesture of street-opulence, only the Poya moon that night familiar.

Trains to Polonnaruwa from Colombo on the horizon, to monuments in stone.

Blind to the violet waves of this country: fake flowers at airports, love cake, ayubowans.

Little girls in white uniforms amble past mosques and churches, holding hands.

In the south-west monsoon, thunderstorms in Colombo are not what you imagine.

Piranha

I began to learn it as a child one summer. To the gentle ears of my girl-self it sounded like the refrain of an epic song: உங்களுக்கு பொறாமையா? Around that time, petty rivalry seemed to feature in the conversation of the adults around me; the Kanjivaram sari of one woman would evoke the envious sentiments of another, a newly purchased home in Surrey unleashed in a man both bitterness and suspicion. My aunts spoke of it in their mother tongue as *poraama*, jealousy, which I misheard as a girl for *piranha*. Perhaps I understood in my little body that jealousy was a predatory disposition. I too would be asked whether I was jealous of a whole manner of incidents—the friendly affection shown to girl-cousins by my grandfather, my mother's beauty at a New Year's party, which at six years of age I feared I did not possess. உங்களுக்கு பொறாமையா? One day, rather than a question, I began to understand it as an instruction. I collected these bone-toothed creatures. Kept them in my pockets. Fed them little pieces of chicken flesh and took them with me to school in my ruby-red satchel. If I was so intimate with them surely I thought, I must in fact be one too. See me stand in front of this mirror. Notice this mouth cling onto flesh. Observe the body, a single flash of muscle moving. *Little girl, little girl, what are you thinking? Mass of teeth, frenzy.*

Dis-location

I found my spine
        in an east London
                park.

It had rooted itself
        firmly to a lime
                tree,

white stucco sitting
        starkly upon sage
                green.

It had severed itself
        from my body so
                gently

one midnight in May
        having lost its
                purpose.

Only the faintest scar
        remained like soft
                judgment.

I found it conversing
        with the local mafia of
                pigeons

and a dog ran up
        to lick along its
                ridge.

I cradled my spine like
        a new-born against my
                cheek

noting the sinuous
        arteries which had
                withered.

I took it by its hand and
        walked it home. The
                police horses

looked at me, flicking
        their hair with a
                knowing gesture.

As I tucked my spine into
        bed I pleaded and cooed
                please, my darling,

don't leave me.
        But the next morning
                it had again left.

I stumbled back to the park.
                    This time
                                  it refused to move:

forget   me
              like I will   surely
                            forget you.

surely forget   me
              like   you   will
                            forget.

like I will surely
              forget   you,
                          for me.

At dusk I walked back
              to my flat kicking
                            a grey stone and

collapsed.

Neruda's Last Word(s)
to the woman who collected his shit

it was the dutiful ceremony	of an indifferent queen
an ignoble routine never repeated	she was right to despise me
the most beautiful woman	yet seen in Ceylon
completely unresponsive	it was the coming together
of a man and a statute	her eyes wide open all the while
tiny red dots so very slim	soon naked in my bed
she was another kind of existence	a shy jungle animal a piece of silk
with the steps of a goddess	strong grip on her wrist
stared into her eyes dark beauty	solemnly toward the latrine
one morning no language	I decided to go all the way

Language found in Pablo Neruda's Memoirs *(1977)*

period party / புண்ணியதானம்

a *big girl* now / fathers and mothers
rush / to tell the news to uncles and aunties
of her bloodletting / stories of a daughter's body travel fast /
otherwise unaccommodated /

*

I've been wanting to write a poem about the ritual ceremony that girls in my Tamil community are often made to participate in when they get their first period. I'd been unable to write that poem, afraid to confront the shame I still experienced in my own body. I was naively optimistic that such things were no longer being practised. Earlier this year however, I received an invitation to attend the puberty ceremony of the child of a family friend.

*

her skin is soft buttermilk / breasts
tender from the effort of first growth / walking
with hunched shoulders, nipples protruding / pink lace lines
her first bra / the brown stain on her cream nightie / changes
everything / nothing / she still watches Neighbours on
Saturday mornings / but doesn't want to hold her mumma's
hand anymore / she tiptoes the aisles of supermarkets to buy
sanitary napkins / new emotional consciousness arrests her /
the false bravado of thirteen-year-old-girls learning about
childbirth and sexual education / the physical response to the
sound of *men* and *rape* /

*

If you search 'period party' on Google, you enter the world of professional puberty celebration planning. This is particularly popular in parts of the world where there is a concentration of Tamil people, like South India, Germany, France and England. There are YouTube videos where girls of eleven, twelve, thirteen years of age are taken through a ceremony which resembles a wedding. Can a girl of twelve consent to the announcement of her period? It is confusing for me that some girls say they look forward to experiencing the ceremony. The ritual has its roots in a time when a girl's first period would mark the sign of the beginning of her sexual life and availability for marriage. If you look closely at the girls' smiling faces in the videos, it is like watching a strange mime.

*

the girl / the girl bleeds / the girl bleeds over and over / you live to see this girl bleed over and over / yet, she lives /

Notes on Lunar Theory

I. Avoid reading your birth-chart on your Blackberry.

II. For optimal viewing of planetary positions, iPhones and Android are best.

III. *Just £4.99!* to read your horoscope on tamastroguru.com.

IV. Be patient—you will be informed eventually of whom you will marry, on what date you will die and under whose foot you must avoid being buried.

V. Mourn the eventual loss of your youthful body.

VI. Your daughter will be born in seven years. Name her Padmini பத்மினி, *the one who is adrift upon a lotus.*

VII. Her skin will be like charcoal. You will relish its beauty. Yours is the colour of the curd your mother fed you.

VIII. One day your daughter will show you her palms, wet with alta, and you will trace your fingers along them.

IX. Recite the mantra three times to avoid death.

X. The priest refuses to tell you its words. You retrieve them from his bloodied tongue, anyway.

XI. Notice your daughter's strong heart. You can see it right there in the corner quadrant of the chart, adjacent to your own.

Brihadeeswar

I smell the gods   before I catch sight of their form   black stone yoni and lingam   bathed in pink petals, coconut oil

There is no water in this city   the river Kaveri   is so dry
     its bridges are lonely twigs

I visit the temple first with mother   and later with father
our feet scald   walking across the hot stones   *we long for rain*

The scriptures are muddled in my brain   the verbs and tenses unruly
     remember   *you must learn to love mud*   *& eat mortality*

Mother and I look up at the shikara from inside
     it is not about religion thangam   it is about the resilience of stone

The marigolds in my palms wilt   a single ant
     crawls along the spine of the banana   given as prasadam

Mother and I laze on our back in the hotel room   and listen to
     AR Rahman   the sun turns everything outside to dust

She holds my wrist finally and slips two gold bangles   enclasped with
the heads of snakes   one on each arm   *and so we rotate*

One Hundred and Eight Commands for My Daughter

Kālī on the Battlefield

I.

Darling girl, it's strange how the sound
you most relate with time is that of a clock.

As if such banality   tick   tock   tick   tock
the sound of a nursery rhyme—

could obscure its true nature.

II.

Last night, we stumbled through languid rivers
and bloated mountains.

Blackberries rolled on our tongues to sate hunger.

We stalked cities and pocketed jade, golden anklets
and ruby amulets as our dreams clipped our heels.

III.

We arrived to the ugly mouth of this country,
unmet by vermillion on our black skin and surveyed the land.

To its decayed fringes we walked and mingled
with lost girls, carrion, ghosts. We were home.

Home: the only place where pain and shame
stand idle next to tenderness.

IV.

Our feet traced the red clay of the earth
and we stood in the centre of a circle of women

who conversed with the spirits
of beautiful girls on pyres

who say:

beauty has its own logic but   *so does decay*

                                                     so does subversion

                                                   so does destruction

V.

Daughter, when you think of eternity what does it feel
like in your chest?

Remember all this when you take my place.

VI.

Come, listen—put your ear to this, a broken radio,
presented to me by a small slip of a girl, emitting sounds from space.

It calls out my name, all one thousand and eight of them

lolā   *līlā*   *kāmada*   *kāminī*

sulocanā   *trilocanā*   *sarasvatī*

The one who is desired. The one who desires herself.

VII.

And in the end, on the battlefield, only we will remain.

Mothers will no longer burn,
the moon gravitates towards the sea.

Tongues will curl into throats—my body, your body will fold.

VIII.

Why are you just standing there, darling?

Take this knife.

It's time.

Notes

'Girl, Ceylon' derives its title from the photograph of the same name by Julia Margaret Cameron. Reference was made to Julian Cox and Colin Ford, *Julia Margaret Cameron: Complete Photographs*, 2002, Getty Publications, for details about the albumen photographic process.

'sea level' uses the word for 'sea' or a large body of water from different languages.

In 'Piranha', the phrases in Tamil ask the question: *are you jealous?*

'One Hundred and Eight Commands for My Daughter' appeared as 'Black Lullaby' in Season 1 of *Bedtime Stories for the End of the World*.

Image credits

Page 13: Julia Margaret Cameron (British, born India, 1815 - 1879), *Girl, Ceylon*, 1875–1879, Albumen silver print, The J. Paul Getty Museum, Los Angeles. Digital image courtesy of the Getty's Open Content Program.

Page 29: The Hindu Goddess Durga, India, Himachal Pradesh, Basohli, late 17th century, Los Angeles County Museum of Art: www.lacma.org. *Image altered from original.*

Cover imagery collages *Girl, Ceylon*, Julia Cameron (details above) with *blue ocean waves* by Photo Junction/Shutterstock.com

Acknowledgements

This book is a product of so much love and generosity shown to me, the good fortune of a large and loving family, wonderful teachers and access to libraries, books and opportunities. I also gratefully acknowledge the writers of previous generations, particularly women of colour, who paved the way for me to write.

I would like to thank Amy Acre and Jake Wild Hall for their support and for being such wonderful publishers. A special thank you to Amy for being a brilliant editor and designer.

Thank you to the editors and publishers of *The Good Journal, Bedtime Stories for the End of the World, amberflora, Poetry Birmingham Literary Journal, harana poetry* and *ZARF* in which some poems, or versions of them, previously appeared.

I am grateful to Poetry London, Spread the Word, The Poetry School and 3 of Cups Press for supporting my work and for providing space for writing to flourish.

Thank you to Mona Arshi, Will Harris, Mimi Khalvati and Shivanee Ramlochan—generous and masterful poets—whose workshops I attended.

Thank you to everyone who read earlier versions of the poems and who continue to provide warm support and encouragement particularly SK Grout, Gurmeet Kaur, Alice Hiller, Tanatsei Gambura, Yomi Ṣode, the Convent Garden Stanza community and the Foxglove poets.

Eternal and the most gratitude always for my family, parents and friends. Especially my brothers, athai Sivajothy, mum Vasuki and ammai Saraswathy. Thank you to Murali.

In memory of Dr Veerappapillai Somasundaram (1941- 2020)

Lightning Source UK Ltd.
Milton Keynes UK
UKHW012335100621
385294UK00002B/122